Easy Game Cookery

by Phyllis Hobson

A successful hunt should mean good eating at the table, not hard work in the kitchen. The best ways to cook game are the easiest.

One of the best recipes for venison can be written in one sentence: Roast the haunch on a spit over an open fire with a little salt and pepper and an occasional basting of butter. There are other easy ways you can bake and simmer and sauté wild game without qualifying as a gourmet cook. Cooking game need not be dull, just easy.

That is the key word for the best in wild game cookery: easy. Take it easy cooking game. Simmer the meat slowly over low heat. Bake it in a low-to-moderate oven. Fry it gently. Take it easy on the heat. And with these recipes to guide you, sit back and take it easy while the game slowly cooks to its tender, juicy best.

Basic Techniques

For best flavor, game animals should be skinned, game birds plucked, and fish scaled or skinned as soon as possible. The entrails should be removed and the meat washed and chilled. You may want to take large game animals to a butcher or a locker plant for processing. With smaller game, chances are you will do it yourself.

1

All fat should be trimmed from the meat. Although most game animals do not develop the heavy layer of fat characteristic of domestic livestock, their fat is strong tasting and even a small amount will affect the flavor of the meat. The trimmed meat can be basted with cooking oil, butter, or margarine. Ground meat can be mixed with pork or beef fat.

Large and small animals and game birds (but not fish) should be aged to improve the flavor and tenderize the meat. Small game animals and game birds should be wrapped in a damp towel or put in a plastic bag and kept in the refrigerator for a few days to age. One to two days will age young animals and up to four days is good for older, tougher meat. In cold weather, large game may be hung in a cold garage or unheated basement where the temperature does not go above 40 degrees F. Or, the carcass can be cut into large chunks and stored in a refrigerator.

After aging, large game should be cut into roasts, steaks, stew meat, and so on. Small animals and game birds may be cut up or left whole.

The more tender cuts from young game animals can be fried, broiled, sautéed, or cooked on the open grill — just as you would the steaks and chops of beef, pork, and lamb. To fry the steaks, dredge the pieces in flour, season with salt and pepper, and brown in heated oil over low heat. Turn once to brown on both sides and let the meat slowly cook to tender goodness.

Smaller pieces of boneless meat can be sautéed in hot butter or margarine over medium heat. Stir frequently and do not flour. Either way, be careful not to overcook game. Otherwise, it will become tough and dry.

The meat from older animals should be braised or stewed to break down and tenderize the fiber. To braise, first fry or sauté to brown the meat, then add 1/2 to 1 cup liquid, cover, and cook over very low heat until tender, adding small amounts of liquid if necessary.

Meat from more mature game and the tougher cuts from young animals can be fried if they are first tenderized. There are several ways to tenderize meat.

• *Use a commercial tenderizer.* Commercial tenderizers, made from a natural enzyme, will soften the tough muscle tissue in a few minutes. Follow the directions on the package.

- *Marinate.* Place meat slices in a shallow bowl or baking dish and pour over it a coating of French dressing; tomato juice, water, and lemon juice; water and vinegar; or your favorite marinade. Refrigerate 24 hours, turning several times.

- *Pressure-cook.* Stew or braise at 15 pounds of pressure for 15–20 minutes, following the manufacturer's directions.

- *Break down the fiber.* Tenderize by pounding with a meat mallet, chopping, or grinding the meat.

- *Parboil.* Simmer for 15 minutes over low heat in just enough water to cover. Then discard the water and bake, fry, or braise. Parboiling also removes some of the gamey taste from strongly flavored meat.

About that gamey taste. Most people like it — once they have acquired the taste. It is like ripe olives or Limburger cheese; few people like it the first time. But for many people, the different flavor of game is the reason they look forward to the opening of the hunting season. They welcome the change from the monotony of beef, pork, and chicken on the dinner table. If you have not yet acquired the taste, there are ways you can minimize the strong flavor of wild game. Here are a few.

- *Soak it.* Cover the meat with water in which 3 tablespoons of salt or 3 tablespoons of vinegar have been mixed. Soak the meat for 30 minutes. Be careful, though; soaking too long can make the meat soft and watery.

- *Disguise it.* Baste a roast with marinade or gravies rich with garlic or spices. Serve steaks and roasts with flavorful sauces and gravies.

- *Stuff it.* Fill the cavity of whole animals with sliced onions or orange halves. Discard the stuffing after baking.

- *Combine it.* Make stew or ground meat with half game and half beef or pork. Cook a venison stew or pot roast with potatoes and carrots.

- *Parboil it.* Simmer the meat in water before frying or baking. Discard the cooking water.

- *Hunt early in the season.* The meat of large game animals becomes much stronger in taste with the approach of the mating season.

Small Game

Skin the small game as the illustration indicates. When the skin has been removed, cut the abdomen just through the muscle and remove the entrails, being careful not to burst the bile sac. Save the heart and liver and discard the rest. Wash the carcass under running water, wrap in a damp towel, and refrigerate — 1 day for young animals and up to 4 days for older animals.

Small game may be fried, braised, or baked whole or cut in serving pieces. Tougher cuts and meat from older animals should be cooked as you would older chickens.

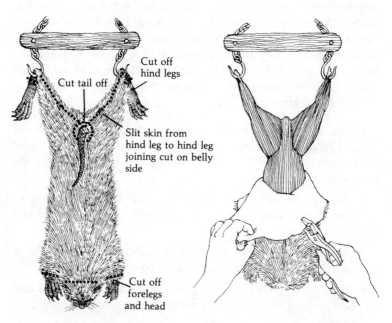

The process of skinning a muskrat can be adapted to any small game. (1.) Cut off the head, tail, and forelegs. (2.) Cut just through the skin around the hock of each leg. (3.) Hang the animal by the hind legs (or fasten it to a table). (4.) Slit the skin from the hind leg to hind leg and foreleg to foreleg through the neck opening. (5.) Working from the top, fold the skin over and peel it off, wrong side out, as you would a tight sweater.

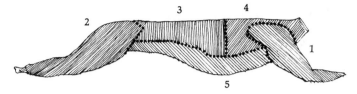

Cut up your small game in the sequence shown.

Rabbit

Rabbit meat is fine grained and mild flavored. The meat of young animals can be used as a substitute for chicken fryers. Meat from older animals needs slow, moist cooking to make it tender.

RABBIT WITH VEGETABLES

1 wild rabbit, cleaned and cut up
1/4 cup flour
1 teaspoon salt
1 teaspoon curry powder
 dash of paprika
1/4 cup cooking oil
4 small potatoes, scrubbed but unpeeled
4 whole carrots, scrubbed and cut into 3-inch lengths
1 small onion, sliced
1 cup water
1 bay leaf
 salt and pepper
3 tablespoons flour
1/2 cup cold water

Dredge rabbit pieces in flour mixed with salt, curry powder, and paprika. Brown in hot oil in a heavy skillet. Cover and bake for 30 minutes at 350 degrees F. Add vegetables, water, and bay leaf. Season with salt and pepper. Cover and bake another hour. Remove meat and vegetables to serving dish. Discard bay leaf.

Blend 3 tablespoons flour and 1/2 cup water and gradually add to liquid. Cook, stirring constantly, until thickened. Pour over meat and vegetables. Serves 4–6

JUGGED HARE

1 wild rabbit, cut up
1/2 cup flour
salt and pepper
2 tablespoons cooking oil
1 small onion
6 whole cloves
1 bay leaf
1 small bunch parsley
1 small bunch marjoram
1 small bunch thyme
1 lemon, thinly sliced
4 cups seasoned beef or chicken stock, or 4 cups water and 4 beef or
   chicken bouillon cubes
1 cup red wine

Dredge the rabbit pieces in flour, season with salt and pepper, and lightly brown in hot oil.

Pack the browned pieces as tightly as possible in a wide-mouth canning jar, coffee can, or pudding steamer. Stud the onion with the cloves and add to the jar. Combine the bay leaf, parsley, marjoram, and thyme in a piece of cheesecloth. Tie with a string and add to jar. Top with lemon slices, stock, and wine. Cover with a tight-fitting lid or a piece of aluminum foil tied in place.

Set the container in a pan with 4 inches of boiling water. Steam for 2 hours. An old favorite of herb enthusiasts, Jugged Hare can be served hot or cold and keeps well in the refrigerator for late night snacks. Serves 4–6.

SOME TIPS

It's a good idea to wear rubber gloves when skinning or cleaning any game animal. Never, never dress an animal that looks sick or in poor condition. Bury it, as soon and as deeply as possible, without touching it.

Squirrel

Squirrel meat is similar to rabbit except it has a stronger flavor. Most rabbit recipes can be used for squirrel. If the animal is old, simmer it in gravy until tender.

SQUIRREL SKILLET PIE

1 squirrel, cleaned and cut up
1/2 teaspoon salt
water to barely cover
1/2 cup celery, chopped
1/4 cup butter or margarine
1/4 cup minced onion
1/4 cup sweet red or green pepper, chopped
1/4 cup flour
salt and pepper
2 packages canned, ready-to-bake biscuits

Cover squirrel pieces with salted water. Add chopped celery, cover, and simmer until the meat is tender. Remove the meat, but save the cooking liquid. When the meat has cooled, pull it from the bones, leaving it in fairly large pieces. Set aside.

In a large iron skillet, melt better or margarine over low heat. Add onion and peppers and cook about 5 minutes, until onion is transparent but not browned. Blend in flour and cook until the mixture bubbles, stirring constantly. Pour in 2 cups cooking liquid. Cook until thick and smooth, stirring constantly. Season to taste with salt and pepper. Add meat and reheat to boiling. Top with canned biscuits and bake at 350 degrees F. for 10–12 minutes, until biscuits are browned. Serves 4–6.

Opossum

Opossum is a rich food; and it is not for everyone. But to those who like it, there is nothing better than roast 'possum. It was once a staple of the winter months in the South.

BARBECUED OPOSSUM

1 whole opossum, cleaned
2 quarts cold water
1 teaspoon salt
1 small hot pepper
1 cup barbecue sauce

Cover whole opossum with cold water. Add salt and hot pepper and simmer over low heat for 30 minutes, just until tender. Discard cooking water and place opossum in a baking pan. Bake at 350 degrees F. until crisp and golden, basting frequently with barbecue sauce. Serves 6.

Porcupine

Skin a porcupine just as you would a rabbit. Dress it and wipe with a damp cloth. The meat is especially good with this unusual stuffing.

STUFFED PORCUPINE

1 whole porcupine, cleaned and dressed
salt and pepper
3 cups sauerkraut
1 apple, cored and coarsely chopped
2 tablespoons melted butter or margarine

Sprinkle porcupine inside and out with salt and pepper. Stuff lightly with sauerkraut mixed with chopped apple. Truss or sew up and place in an uncovered baking pan. Bake at 350 degrees F. for 1-1-1/2 hours, until tender, brushing frequently with melted butter or margarine. Serves 4-6.

Raccoon

Skin and dress a freshly killed raccoon. Carefully remove the brown, bean-shaped kernels under each front leg and on both sides of the spine. Wipe with a cloth dipped in vinegar and water.

ROAST RACCOON

1 raccoon, cleaned and cut up
1/2 cup flour
1 teaspoon salt
1/4 teaspoon pepper
1/4 cup cooking oil
2 medium onions, peeled and sliced
2 bay leaves

Dredge the meaty pieces of raccoon in flour that has been seasoned with salt and pepper. Brown pieces on both sides in cooking oil in a heavy skillet. Pour off excess oil. Add onions and bay leaves and cover. Bake at 350 degrees F. for 2 hours, until tender.

Simmer bony pieces in water to cover until tender. Strain and season the broth, then use it to make gravy. Serves 6.

Muskrat

A very clean animal, the muskrat feeds only on plants and roots, which gives the meat a sweet flavor. It tends to be soft, though, and should be crisply fried.

CRISPY
FRIED MUSKRAT

1 muskrat, cleaned and cut up
2 eggs, well beaten
1 tablespoon milk
2 cups commercial biscuit mix
1/2 cup catsup
3/4 cup cooking oil

Cut muskrat as you would rabbit or squirrel. Use only the meaty pieces. Reserve the bony pieces for soup or gravy. Dry pieces with a paper towel, then dip in eggs mixed with milk. Dip in biscuit mix, then in catsup, and again in biscuit mix. Fry in heated oil until crisp and golden brown. Serves 4-6.

Woodchuck

When skinning a woodchuck, take care to remove the red scent glands between the forelegs and the body. Because of its strong flavor, woodchuck should be parboiled in salt water for 20 minutes before baking or using in this recipe.

WOODCHUCK CASSEROLE

1 woodchuck, cleaned, parboiled, and cut up
1 teaspoon salt
1/8 teaspoon pepper
1 teaspoon ground thyme
4 large bay leaves
8 slices bacon
1 cup water
1 cup dry bread crumbs
1/2 teaspoon seasoned salt

Arrange a layer of meat in an oiled casserole. Combine salt, pepper, and thyme and sprinkle half the mixture over the meat. Lay 2 bay leaves and 4 bacon slices over the top. Repeat layer. Pour 1 cup water over all. Cover and bake at 350 degrees F. for 1–2 hours, until tender. Remove lid and sprinkle with bread crumbs, then seasoned salt. Bake 30 minutes longer, uncovered. Serves 4–6.

Large Game

The method of cleaning and skinning large game is the same as for small animals, although larger animals are more difficult to hang and skin because of their size.

Hang the animal by the hind legs in a cool place as soon as possible after killing. To skin the carcass, cut around each of the ankles, and pull the legs through. Cut off the head and feet and discard. Strip the skin from the hind legs down, carefully cutting it away as you go.

To clean, slit the flesh up the front from the tail to the throat and take out the entrails. Remove the bile sac from the liver without bursting the sac. Refrigerate the heart and liver and discard the other entrails.

Wipe the carcass thoroughly inside and out with a cloth dipped in a solution of 1 cup water and 1 tablespoon vinegar.

FIELD DRESSING YOUR DEER

Dress your deer immediately after tagging. Roll the deer over on its back, rump lower than shoulders, and spread the hind legs. Cut along the centerline of belly from breastbone to base of tail. First, cut through the hide, then through the belly muscle. Avoid cutting into the paunch and intestines by holding them away from the knife with the free hand while guiding the knife with the other.

With a small, sharp knife, cut around the anus. Tie off with cord and draw it into the body cavity so it comes free with the complete intestines. In doing this, avoid cutting or breaking the bladder. Loosen and roll out the stomach and intestines along with the genital organs. Save the liver if desired. Cut around the edge of the diaphragm which separates the chest and stomach cavities, then reach forward to cut the windpipe and gullet ahead of the lungs. This should allow you to pull the lungs and heart from the chest cavity. Save the heart if desired. Drain all blood from the body cavity.

From *Dressing Out Your Deer*, Special Circular 119, The Pennsylvania State University, College of Agriculture Extension Service, University Park, PA.

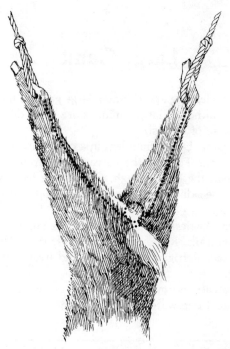

To skin a large game animal: (1) With the animal hanging by the hocks, cut off the head, tail, and all four feet. (2) Slit the skin between the hind legs, and between the two forelegs, and down the center of the belly. (3) With a sharp knife, cut around anus to loosen it. (4) Using a skinning knife, work the skin loose from the hind legs and begin to peel it off. Work the skin down, pulling it away from the carcass and cutting away any tissue.

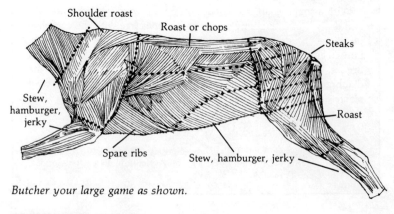

Butcher your large game as shown.

Let the meat hang at a temperature of 35–40 degrees F. for 1–2 weeks. This aging process tenderizes the meat and gives it flavor. The meat now is ready to be cut according to the illustration. The following are easy recipes that can be used for any large game.

ROAST GAME

4 tablespoons cooking oil
1 tablespoon vinegar
1/4 cup catsup
2 tablespoons Worcestershire sauce
1 clove of garlic, chopped

Combine all ingredients. Cover and refrigerate overnight. Use as a basting sauce for roasting any large game roast. Bake at 250 degrees F. 4–6 hours, basting frequently.

WOODMAN'S STEW

2 pounds lean, boned meat, cut in 1-inch cubes
1 cup flour
1 teaspoon salt
1/8 teaspoon pepper
1/2 cup cooking oil
2 cups water
2 cloves garlic, minced
1 medium onion, chopped
4 tablespoons vinegar
1 teaspoon grated lemon rind
2 tablespoons Worcestershire sauce

Dredge meat cubes in flour mixed with salt and pepper. Brown on all sides in heated cooking oil in a Dutch oven. Remove the meat, and to the fat in the pan add 3 tablespoons flour left from dredging. Stir in well, then add remaining ingredients. Return meat to gravy and cook over low heat (or a campfire) 1-1/2–2 hours, until tender. Serves 6 at home or 4 in the woods.

EASY GAME MINCEMEAT

Here is a way to make use of the bones left over after butchering any large game animal. Even well-trimmed bones have a lot of meat on them.

bones from freshly butchered large game
2 quarts water
3/4 pound beef fat
3 pounds apples; peeled, quartered, and cored
1 whole lemon, unpeeled
1 whole orange, unpeeled
3 pounds seedless raisins
1 pound dried currants
1 pound brown sugar
1 teaspoon powdered allspice
1 tablespoon salt
1 tablespoon powdered cinnamon
1 tablespoon powdered ginger
1 tablespoon powdered cloves
1 tablespoon powdered nutmeg
2 quarts apple cider

Cook bones in 2 quarts of water in a pressure canner at 15 pounds pressure for 30 minutes, or in a large kettle with water to cover for 3–4 hours. Remove bones from broth and cool. Strain broth, reserving both meat and liquid. Save liquid for soup or gravy.

Pick meat from bones, add to strained meat, and put through the coarse blade of a food chopper or food processor. There should be 2 cups of meat. Grind beef fat, apples, lemon and orange (remove any seeds), raisins, and currants. Add remaining ingredients and simmer over very low heat for 2 hours, stirring frequently to keep from sticking. This recipe makes 5 or 6 pints of mincemeat and 1 pint makes 1 medium-sized pie.

Venison

Although usually thought of as deer meat, venison is the meat from any antlered game animal, including deer, caribou, elk, and moose.

The meat from young animals is tender, with a mild flavor. It is cooked as you would cook beef. The texture is similar to veal or beef; but without the marbled fat of beef, it tends to be dry.

The meat from old animals or mature bucks during the mating season may be tough or strong tasting and should be marinated or basted with barbecue sauce.

The following recipes can be used interchangeably with any antlered game.

VENISON STEW

2-3 pounds venison roast, cut in 1-inch cubes
1/2 cup flour
1 teaspoon salt
1/8 teaspoon pepper
1/4 cup cooking oil
2 cups boiling water
1 bay leaf
2 beef bouillon cubes
12 small whole onions, peeled
6 medium carrots, peeled and cut into 2-inch chunks
1 package frozen green lima beans
3 tablespoons flour
1/2 cup cold water
2 large green peppers, seeded and cut in rings

Dredge venison cubes in flour that has been mixed with salt and pepper. Brown on all sides in cooking oil. Add boiling water and bay leaf. Cover and simmer over low heat for 30 minutes. Discard bay leaf. Add bouillon cubes, onions, and carrots. Simmer 45 minutes longer. Stir in lima beans and cook for an additional 15 minutes.

With a slotted spoon, remove meat and vegetables to a serving dish, leaving cooking liquid in the pan. Blend 3 tablespoons flour and 1/2 cup cold water in a cup and gradually add to hot liquid. Cook, stirring constantly, until smooth and thickened. Pour over meat and vegetables. Top with green pepper rings. Broil 5 minutes, until browned on top. Serves 6.

VENISON SAUERBRATEN

1 large venison roast
2 medium onions, chopped
2 bay leaves
12 peppercorns
6 whole cloves
2 teaspoons salt
1 cup apple cider
1/2 cup cider vinegar
1 cup boiling water
1/4 cup cooking oil
12 gingersnap cookies, crushed
2 teaspoons brown sugar

In a large mixing bowl, cover venison with a mixture of onions, bay leaves, peppercorns, cloves, salt, cider, vinegar, and boiling water. Cover tightly and refrigerate 3–7 days, turning meat several times a day. The day before serving, drain meat and strain the liquid, discarding onions and seasonings. Brown meat in oil in a Dutch oven or crock pot. Add strained liquid, cover, and cook over low heat for 3–4 hours in a Dutch oven, or 12–24 hours in a crock pot. Remove meat to platter. Turn heat to high over cooking liquid and add the gingersnaps and sugar. Cover and simmer 5 minutes. Serve as a gravy with the meat. Serves 4–6.

CARIBOU CASSEROLE

6 caribou (or other venison) butterfly steaks
salt and pepper
1 package dry onion soup mix
2 fresh tomatoes, quartered
1 can condensed cream of mushroom soup
1 cup milk

Flatten the steaks as thinly as possible with a meat mallet. Arrange in a shallow baking pan. Season with salt and pepper and sprinkle with dry soup mix. Arrange tomatoes evenly around pan. Combine soup and milk and pour over all. Bake, uncovered at 300 degrees F. for 1-1/2 hours, until the meat is brown and tender. Serves 6.

Bear

Bear meat is dark and well flavored. The layer of fat should be trimmed off or it will give the meat a strong gamey taste.

Bear meat, like pork, is a carrier of trichinosis, so it must be cooked to well done (185 degrees F.) or frozen 3–4 weeks before cooking.

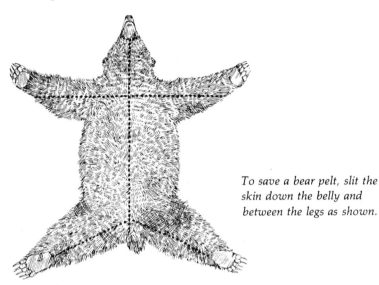

To save a bear pelt, slit the skin down the belly and between the legs as shown.

BEAR STEAKS

1 bear round steak, about 3/4-inch thick
1/2 cup flour
1/2 teaspoon salt
1/8 teaspoon pepper
1/4 cup cooking oil
1 can condensed cream of celery soup
1 cup milk

Trim any fat from steak. Cut in serving-size pieces and sprinkle with flour mixed with salt and pepper. Pound with a meat mallet or the edge of a saucer until all flour is worked into meat. Brown on both sides in hot oil. Combine soup and milk and pour over meat. Cover and bake at 300 degrees F. for 1 hour. Uncover and bake 15 minutes longer. Serves 6.

Wild Boar

The texture and flavor of wild boar meat is much like that of pork, except there is little fat. The meat has a gamey taste because of the animal's diet. Like pork, wild boar must be cooked to well done (185 degrees F.) or frozen 3–4 weeks before cooking.

Boar is cleaned, dressed, and cooked in the same way as pork. Very young animals are barbecued whole.

WILD BOAR ROAST

1 large loin roast of boar, trimmed of fat
1-1/2 teaspoons salt
1/2 teaspoon powdered thyme
1-1/2 teaspoons dry mustard
1/2 teaspoon powdered ginger
1-1/4 cups orange juice
3/4 cup honey
1 unpeeled orange, thinly sliced

Place roast in shallow baking pan. Combine salt, thyme, mustard, and ginger and rub over the meat. Bake 1 hour at 300 degrees F., then baste with 1/4 cup orange juice. Bake 1 hour more, basting 3 more times with 1/4 cup orange juice each time. Combine remaining 1/4 cup orange juice and honey and baste with this mixture. Bake 45 minutes longer or until meat thermometer inserted in center registers 185 degrees F. Baste often with liquid in bottom of the pan. Garnish with orange slices. Serves 6.

MORE INFORMATION

If you are looking for a more detailed description of field dressing and cleaning game and fish, read Bob Candy's *Getting the Most from Your Game & Fish* (Garden Way Publishing). Candy will tell you some very useful tips to enable you to bring home the highest quality meat.

Game Birds

Game birds, like other game animals, should be cleaned as soon as possible after being killed. The entrails are removed after the birds are plucked.

For easier plucking, work quickly, while the bird is still warm. Dip the beheaded bird into a pot of water in which a cake of paraffin has been melted. The water should be hot enough to melt the paraffin, but not hot enough to cook the skin.

Pluck the feathers off in handfuls, singe off the fuzz over an open flame and remove any pinfeathers with a knife or a pair of tweezers. If the bird is to be stewed, it may be easier to skin it.

Game birds should be aged in the refrigerator for 1 day for young, tender birds up to 4 days for older birds.

Roast game bird slowly over an open fire or in a slow oven turning frequently and basting with butter or margarine or your favorite basting sauce.

ROAST WILD GOOSE

2 cups bread crumbs
1/4 cup butter or margarine, melted
1/4 cup chopped orange, peeled
1/4 teaspoon grated orange rind
3/4 cup celery, diced
1 cup cooked pitted prunes, chopped
1/2 teaspoon salt
1 wild goose, cleaned and aged
salt and pepper

Sauté bread crumbs in melted butter or margarine. Add chopped orange, orange rind, celery, prunes, and salt. Stuff goose cavity lightly and place in roasting pan. Sprinkle with salt and pepper. Bake at 300 degrees F. for 1-1/2 hours, basting frequently with pan drippings. Serves 6.

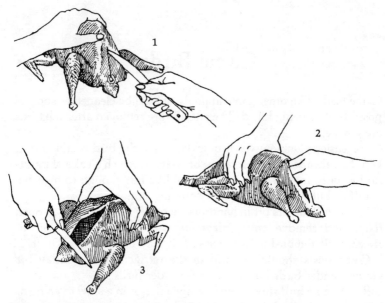

Preparing a game bird is similar to preparing domestic fowl.
1. Slit the skin from vent to breast bone.
2. Reach into the body cavity and remove entrails.
3. Cut off tail.

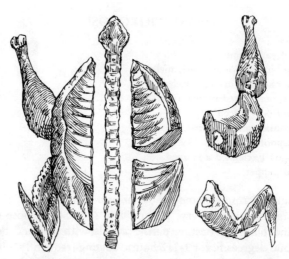

Cut larger game birds into breast pieces, wings, and legs and thighs. The bony back pieces usually are discarded or simmered in water to make soup stock or gravy.

ROAST WILD DUCK

2 wild ducks, cleaned and aged
1 teaspoon salt
1/8 teaspoon pepper
1/4 teaspoon crushed rosemary leaves
1 medium onion, thickly sliced
1 unpeeled apple, cored and sliced
2 stalks (ribs) celery, cut in chunks
1 unpeeled orange, sliced
1/2 cup butter or margarine, melted
1/4 teaspoon pepper
1/4 teaspoon crushed rosemary leaves

Wipe ducks dry. Blend salt, pepper, and rosemary and sprinkle over ducks, inside and out. Combine onion, apple, celery, and orange and stuff each cavity with half the mixture. Put ducks on roasting rack, breast sides down. Roast 30 minutes at 325 degrees F. Combine butter, pepper, and rosemary and baste ducks with this mixture. Roast 1 hour longer, basting occasionally, until tender. Empty cavities and discard contents of ducks before serving. Serves 4–6.

QUAIL ROASTED
IN GRAPE LEAVES

6 dressed quail
4 tablespoons butter or margarine, melted
salt and pepper
12 grape leaves
1 tablespoon water
juice of 1 lemon
6 slices buttered toast

Wipe quail dry. Brush inside and out with 2 tablespoons melted butter or margarine. Sprinkle with salt and pepper. Wrap each bird in 2 grape leaves and place in a baking dish. Bake at 350 degrees F. for 45 minutes, until tender. Arrange toast on platter. Remove birds to platter, discarding grape leaves. Add remaining butter, water, and lemon juice to the pan drippings and simmer over low heat, stirring constantly. Pour over quail on platter. Serves 6.

EASY PARTY PHEASANT

1 pheasant, cleaned, aged, and cut up
1 can condensed cream of mushroom soup
1/2 cup apple cider
1-1/2 tablespoons Worcestershire sauce
1/2 teaspoon salt
2 tablespoons minced onion
1 clove garlic, crushed
1/2 cup fresh mushrooms, sliced
paprika

Place pheasant pieces in baking dish. Combine remaining ingredients, except paprika, and pour over pheasant. Sprinkle with paprika. Bake at 300 degrees F. for 1–1/2 hours, until tender. Serves 4.

RICE-STUFFED GROUSE

2 large grouse, cleaned and aged
1 teaspoon salt
1/8 teaspoon pepper
1-1/2 cups brown or wild rice
1 teaspoon salt
4 cups boiling water
2 tablespoons butter or margarine
1 cup celery, chopped
3 tablespoons minced onion
1/2 cup fresh mushrooms, sliced
pinch of sage
pinch of dried thyme
pinch of dried savory
6 slices bacon

Sprinkle the cavities of the birds with salt and pepper. Refrigerate. Meanwhile, cook the rice in salted water until tender, about 45 minutes. Sauté celery, onion, and mushrooms in melted butter or margarine and add to cooked rice. Stir in herbs. Stuff grouse lightly with the mixture. Place in a baking pan and cover the breasts with bacon slices. Bake at 300 degrees F. for 1-1/2 hours, until tender. Remove bacon during the last 30 minutes of baking. Serves 4–6.

POTTED PIGEONS

2 cups dry bread crumbs
1/2 cup finely chopped celery
2 tablespoons finely chopped onion
2 tablespoons butter or margarine, melted
4 pigeons
4 tablespoons butter or margarine, melted
1 cup chopped celery leaves
1/2 cup chopped onion
1/2 cup carrot slices
1/2 teaspoon salt
1/8 teaspoon pepper
2 cups boiling water
3 tablespoons flour
1/2 cup cold water

Make dressing by combining bread crumbs, celery, onion, and butter. Mix well and stuff cavities of pigeons. Sew cavity with needle and coarse thread. Brown lightly in 4 tablespoons butter or margarine. Arrange in casserole or baking pan. Add celery leaves, onion, carrot slices, salt, pepper, and boiling water. Cover and bake at 300 degrees F. 1-1-1/2 hours, until tender. While pigeons are baking, simmer giblets in water to cover for 10 minutes. Cool and chop fine. Return to cooking stock. Thicken the stock with flour that has been blended with 1/2 cup water. Simmer 5 minutes and pour over pigeons on serving platter. Serves 4.

PHEASANT BAKED IN FOIL

1 pheasant, cleaned and aged
3 tablespoons butter or margarine, melted
1 teaspoon salt
1/8 teaspoon pepper
1/2 unpeeled orange

Dry pheasant and brush with melted butter or margarine. Sprinkle inside and out with salt and pepper. Stuff orange half in cavity. Place pheasant on large sheet of aluminum cooking foil, bring edges together, and seal tightly. Place in roasting pan and bake at 450 degrees F. for 1 hour. Open foil, reduce heat to 350 degrees F. and bake 20 minutes more, until golden brown. Serves 4.

Fish

Most fish must be scaled before cleaning. To make this job easier, first soak the fish for a few minutes in cold water. Then, holding it down firmly, scrape with a dull knife from the tail to the head. Be sure you have removed all the scales near the base of the fins and head.

To clean, use a sharp knife to slit the belly from vent to gills and remove the entrails. Discard. Cut around and remove all fins and cut off the head. Rinse quickly in cold water and wipe dry. Do not soak in water after cleaning.

Small fish usually are cooked whole, with the tail on, but larger fish may be cut crosswise into steaks or lengthwise into fillets.

To cut a boneless fillet, use a sharp knife to cut the meat away from the backbone from the tail to the head. Cut the piece loose and lift the entire side of the fish in one piece. Turn the fish over and repeat the process on the other side. You will have two boneless fillets per fish. The remainder of the fish may be discarded or used for soup.

To skin catfish, nail the fish to a solid surface and cut through the skin around the head. Using a pair of pliers, pull the skin down to the tail. Cut off the head and tail and remove entrails as above.

Cook fish quickly but gently. All fish, regardless of age, are tender and may be baked, poached (never stewed), fried, or broiled. Fish should be cooked over low heat just until the flesh flakes easily with a fork.

BAKED TROUT

1 whole fresh trout, cleaned
lemon juice
salt and pepper

Dip trout in lemon juice and arrange in oiled baking pan. Season with salt and pepper. Bake at 350 degrees F. for 20–30 minutes, until done. Serves 1–2.

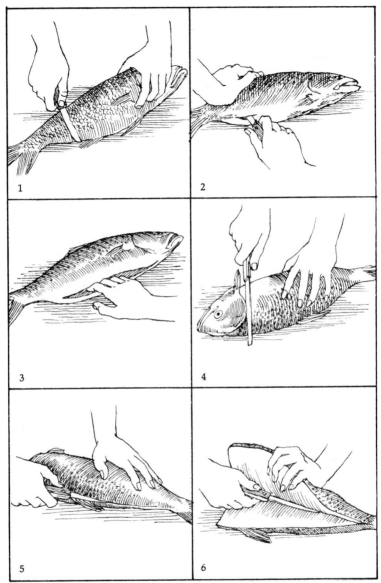

To clean fish:
1. Scrape off scales.
2. Insert knife at vent and slit up to head.
3. Remove entrails
4. Cut off head, fins, and tail.
5. Cut the fillet from head to tail.
6. Cut along backbone from tail to head to remove fillet.

ROLLED FISH FILLETS

1 tablespoon butter or margarine
1 small onion, finely chopped
6–8 fish fillets
salt and pepper
2 cups tomatoes, canned or fresh
1/2 cup fresh mushrooms
1 cup cold water
2 tablespoons butter or margarine
2 tablespoons flour

Melt butter or margarine in skillet. Sauté chopped onion for 2 minutes over low heat, stirring constantly. Spread onion over bottom of skillet. Season fish fillets with salt and pepper and roll them up, jelly-roll style. Arrange rolls in skillet over onions. Top with tomatoes, mushrooms, and water. Simmer 10 minutes, until fish is cooked. Remove fish to platter and cook tomato sauce until it thickens. Season with salt and pepper and thicken with butter and flour that have been blended. Pour over fish on platter. Serves 6.

PICKLED FISH

16 small fish or 4 medium fish, cut into pieces
1 teaspoon salt
water to cover
4 tablespoons cooking oil
1 cup water
1 cup cider vinegar
4 tablespoons minced onion
2 teaspoons mixed pickling spice
1 sweet red pepper, chopped fine
2 teaspoons salt
1/4 teaspoon pepper

Simmer fish in salted water to cover until meat can be flaked with a fork, 8–10 minutes. Cool. Combine remaining ingredients in a bowl with a tight-fitting cover. Add drained fish. Cover and refrigerate, turning 2 or 3 times a day. Fish may be served after 2 days, but it will keep in the refrigerator up to 2 weeks. Serve as a relish, appetizer, or main dish.

FISH BAKED IN MILK

6 whole fish, cleaned and scaled
3 cups hot milk
salt and pepper
3 tablespoons flour
4 tablespoons butter or margarine

Wash fish and wipe dry. Place in baking pan and cover with hot milk. Bake at 350 degrees F. for 20-30 minutes, depending on thickness of fish. Remove fish to platter, sprinkle with salt and pepper. Thicken milk in pan with flour and season with butter and salt and pepper. Pour sauce over fish. Serves 6.

FISH PACKAGES

1 whole, medium-sized fish, cleaned and scaled
1/2 teaspoon salt
1/8 teaspoon pepper
1/2 small onion, thinly sliced
1/2 medium tomato, peeled and sliced
1 teaspoon lemon juice
1 teaspoon cooking oil
1 tablespoon snipped parsley
4 stuffed olives, sliced

Rub fish with salt and pepper and place on a double thickness of cooking foil. Cover fish with onion and tomato slices and sprinkle with lemon juice, oil, and parsley. Top with olive slices. Wrap foil around fish and seal. Bake at 400 degrees F. or grill 4 inches from coals 20-30 minutes. Make 1 package for each serving.

OVEN-FRIED FISH

1/2 cup cooking oil
8 medium fish, cleaned
1 egg, well beaten
1 cup cracker crumbs

Pour oil in baking pan. Heat in a 350 degree F. oven. Dip fish in beaten egg, then in cracker crumbs, and arrange in preheated baking dish. Bake until browned, about 20 minutes. Serves 8.

FISH SOUP

8–10 small fish, cut into 1-inch chunks
4 quarts water
5 sprigs parsley
2 carrots, sliced
2 stalks (ribs) celery, sliced
1 medium onion, chopped
2 lemon slices
2 teaspoons salt
1/8 teaspoon pepper
1 cup cream
2 egg yolks
3 tablespoons chives, minced

In a soup kettle, simmer fish chunks, water, and vegetables 1 hour. Add lemon slices and simmer 5 minutes more. Strain stock and season to taste with salt and pepper. Blend cream, egg yolks, and chives. Pour hot soup over mixture and stir well. Serves 6.

BAKED BASS WITH BACON

6 bass, cleaned and cut into serving pieces
1/2 cup cornmeal
1 teaspoon salt
1 teaspoon paprika
6 slices bacon

Dip pieces of bass in mixture of cornmeal, salt, and paprika. Place coated pieces in oiled baking dish and top with bacon slices. Bake at 350 degrees F. for 20–30 minutes, until fish is done and bacon is crisp. Serves 6–8.

Miscellaneous Water Game

Some of these recipes are not for the squeamish, but eels and snails and snakes are foods our ancestors ate and other cultures still eat with relish. Crawfish has long been known as "the poor man's lobster," and in Europe snails are a gourmet delicacy.

Crawfish

MOCK LOBSTER

4 quarts water
2 teaspoons salt
1 onion, chopped
1 stalk (rib) celery, chopped
1/2 teaspoon chopped dill weed
30–36 large, live crawfish

Combine ingredients and heat to boiling. Drop in live crawfish and boil hard for 5 minutes. Turn off heat and let crawfish cool in the water. Remove and discard water and vegetables. Before serving, pull out tail fin and intestinal vein. Reheat and serve in the shell with melted butter on the side.

Turtles

Turtles are precooked before they are used in a recipe. To precook, plunge the live turtle in a kettle of boiling water. Boil for 10 minutes. Plunge into ice water. Rub the skin from the legs, tail, and head. Rinse and cover with boiling water and cook another 30 minutes. Remove turtle, lay it on its back to cool.

Cut the undershell loose and remove the meat. Cut the meat, including the leg meat, into small pieces, with the bone in. Cover with cold water and add 1 teaspoon salt; 1 medium onion, sliced; 2 carrots, sliced; 1/2 cup celery, chopped; 1 bay leaf; and 2 whole cloves. Cover and simmer 30 minutes more.

TURTLE STEW

1 cup fresh mushrooms, sliced
2 tablespoons butter or margarine
1 can condensed cream of mushroom soup
1 cup milk
2 cups cooked turtle meat

Sauté mushrooms in butter or margarine for 5 minutes, stirring frequently. Add soup and milk. Stir well and season to taste. Add turtle meat. Serve hot on biscuits or toast. Serves 4–6.

Snakes

Skin snake, remove head and entrails as for eel. See illustration on page 32. Cut into serving-size pieces.

FRENCH FRIED RATTLESNAKE

1 rattlesnake, cleaned and cut up
2 eggs, well beaten
1 clove garlic, minced fine
1 cup cracker crumbs
1/4 cup flour
1 teaspoon salt
1/8 teaspoon pepper
hot oil for deep frying

Dip pieces of snake meat in beaten egg to which garlic has been added. Combine cracker crumbs, flour, salt, and pepper in a paper bag. Drop egg-coated pieces, one at a time, into the bag. Remove and fry until golden brown in hot oil. Serves 4–6.

Frogs

The hind legs of the frog have a delicate fishy-chicken taste. The tender meat is eaten like a chicken drumstick, which it resembles. To clean frog legs, remove the legs from the body and cut off the feet. Peel off the skin. Only the hind legs are eaten.

SCALLOPED FROG LEGS

8 pairs frog legs
1/2 cup flour
salt and pepper
1/2 cup butter or margarine
3 cups milk

Dredge frog legs in flour that has been mixed with salt and pepper. Arrange the legs in a baking pan in which butter or margarine has been melted, turning each piece over to coat with butter on both sides. Pour milk into bottom of pan. Bake at 350 degrees F. for 1-1-1/2 hours, until legs are browned and gravy has formed in bottom of pan. Serves 4.

Snails

STUFFED ESCARGOTS

24–30 snails
1/2 cup salt
2 quarts cold water
1 quart boiling water
2 packages dry vegetable soup mix
1/2 cup butter or margarine, creamed
1/4 cup finely chopped celery
1 teaspoon finely chopped onion
1 clove garlic, crushed
1/4 teaspoon salt
dash of pepper
1/2 cup finely crushed crumbs

Soak snails in salt and cold water 3–4 hours, then rinse in fresh cold water. Cover with fresh cold water and heat. Simmer for 30 minutes. Cool and remove snails from shells. Add boiling water to dry soup mix and gently simmer snails in the soup for 3 hours. Meanwhile, wash half the shells thoroughly. Drain. Stuff each shell with 2 cooked snails and pack with a well-blended mixture of the butter, celery, onion, garlic, salt, and pepper. Place stuffed shells in baking pan and sprinkle each with bread crumbs. Bake at 400 degrees F. for 20 minutes. Serve with a tiny fork or pick. Serves 6.

Eels

To clean freshly caught eels, fasten the eel to a firm surface. Cut around the skin just below the head. Using a pair of pliers, peel the skin off the entire length of the body. Remove the head, cut the body open, and remove the entrails. Wash well. Remove the fins with a pair of scissors and cut off the flesh on both sides of the backbone, forming 2 boneless fillets. Discard backbone and cut fillets into 3-inch pieces. One eel will serve 2–3 persons.

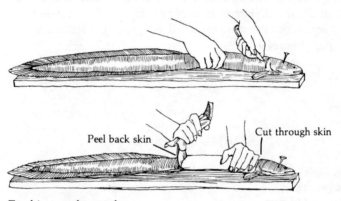

Peel back skin   Cut through skin

To skin an eel or snake:
1. Nail the eel to a board.
2. Cut through the skin just behind head.
3. Grasp the skin firmly and peel the skin back.

EEL-ZUCCHINI CASSEROLE

1 medium eel, cleaned and cut into pieces
2 or 3 immature zucchini, 6–8 inches long
1 medium onion, thinly sliced
4 tablespoons cooking oil
salt and pepper
2 fresh tomatoes, cut into eighths

Sauté eel, zucchini, and onion in cooking oil until the onions are transparent and the eel is browned. Salt and pepper to taste. Add tomatoes. Lower heat, cover, and simmer 30–40 minutes. Stir occasionally, being careful not to break up vegetables. Serves 4.

The Perfect Food Garden Book For Those With Limited Space!

- Wonderfully novel growing ideas for containers. tubs, patios, window sills, sidewalk borders, tiers, all sorts of places!
- Garden plans galore for the most pinched of city and suburban lots: vines on trellises (cucumbers, squashes, tomatoes, beans and more!), herbs and cherry tomatoes in hanging baskets, neat raised beds
- "Edible Fences"
- Fruiting Shrubs and Shade Trees and Hedges
- "Not enough space" will never again be a legitimate complaint!
- Midget Vegetable Varieties
- Dwarf Fruit Trees
- Edible Flowers

If you have even a *sliver* of land, invest in this book— **SUCCESS WITH SMALL FOOD GARDENS** Using Special Intensive Methods—and you'll be repaid dozens of times over in food and *great fun!* There's nothing else like this excellent small book in print.

Landscape Your Place With Eatable Plantings!

With the price of food so high and going up constantly, why not make practically every inch of your homesite produce good eating— with fruit and nut trees, vegetable patches front, back and side, berry-bearing hedges, beds, and borders. Such plantings can be every bit as beautiful—while so much more productive and satisfying! Enjoy your home—and life —a whole lot more. Get ahead financially, with more self-reliance and peace of mind!

SPECIAL OFFER!

Send Today for **SUCCESS WITH SMALL FOOD GARDENS** and SAVE $1.00! Regular Price $5.95, Now Only $4.95 with rebate coupon below. Send to: Garden Way Publishing Co., Dept. B123, Charlotte, Vermont 05445.

- - - - - - - - Please detach here & MAIL TODAY! - - - - - - - - -